IT'S NOT SUPPOSED TO MAKE SENSE IT'S MADNESS

BRANDON SITES

RIVER VALLEY PRESS LLC

Copyright in Progress

Published by River Valley Press LLC
Miamisburg, Ohio, USA

This is a work of creative expression. Names, characters,
places, and incidents are either the products of the author's
imagination or are used fictitiously. Any resemblance to actual
people, living or dead, or actual events is purely coincidental.

Cover design by Anze Ban Virant - ABV atelier
design © River Valley Press LLC.

ISBN:
979-8-9932538-1-7
First Edition

to my mother

I love you

Contents

A Miami Valley Story

Introduction

I once bought a typewriter from a man for seventy-five bucks at a gas station in Norfolk, Virginia, from an ad I'd seen on Facebook Marketplace. To say I had writer's block would be to give me the credit of having written anything at all. After months of staring at the dust collecting between the keys, I posted an ad to sell my typewriter.

An old man sent a message and offered to buy it off me for fifty bucks. I agreed and met him at a Starbucks in Chesapeake for the exchange. He said he was going to grab a coffee first. I got one too, and we sat down at a table.

We were the only two people there, other than the graveyard-shift baristas in the back. The sun was starting to go down, and the shop was closing soon. He began sharing stories about writing projects he'd completed throughout his life. He was looking forward to writing something new on the typewriter as an ode to the past. Maybe it would be the last thing he'd write—he said something like that.

He asked what type of work I'd done, what I'd written. I said, "Sorry, sir. It's getting late; I better be heading home soon."

I was ashamed to tell him the truth—
I wasn't a writer.

Until now.

During a manic episode, I wrote hundreds of free verse poems, prose, haiku & journals over the course of six days. This is a collection of my best work from the rollercoaster I was riding. I'd like to invite you into the inner thoughts of a dark time in my life.

I hope you read this book & like one of my poems.

It's Not Supposed to Make Sense. It's Madness.

The thing about being bipolar
is sometimes I believe I can
do anything.

Sometimes I actually do.

It puts me in rooms I have
no business being in.

Then I stop
and look around,
and I'm like –
Wait...

I actually don't like this room.

I don't want to be here anymore.
I'd like a different room, please.

Thanks.

A Picture's Worth a Thousand Words

My father gave me a picture frame
filled with tickets from every ball game.
One day the glass broke.
Tickets sat in the frame for a while,
glass piercing the paper they were printed on.
Time passed by & there the frame sat,
waiting for someone to pick up the pieces.

Pink Socks

Before you wash the laundry
Separate the whites from the darks
They say don't mix the colors
But I prefer pink socks

Trust Fall *(Haiku)*

Climb high if you can
I'll hold the ladder for you
I'm afraid of heights

Pursuit of Hoppiness

The taste of it is why
Not because it hits the hardest
The hoppiness inside
Will ride this high the farthest

IPA, IPA, IPA, IP-Yay

Poor Woman *(Haiku)*

My mother's bedside
Nine-pound baby is coming
Epidural, please

Do Your Thing Girl

there's nothing wrong
with going shopping
at Walmart
in your pajamas
on the first of the month

Perfect Timing

There's a woman at my gym I really like.
Today, I thought about asking her if she'd
like to get a coffee sometime.
The timing is bad, though.
It's 10:30 AM on a Tuesday.
She's going to know I'm unemployed.
She seems so put together.
She must work from home.

Conversations in the Bathroom Mirror

At some point we
have to stop posting
the same pictures
from a better time
of our life &
live in the moment

me projecting

Laundry Day

I ran out of towels
so after my
shower
I dried off with
a t-shirt.

Only wore it once.

Up, Up, Down, Down, Left, Right, Left, Right, B, A, Start

The character in the
game I play is
more handsome
& taller & more
talented than I'll
ever be.

It's exciting
to pretend.

I can
escape
reality
for a while.

Don't Take it on an Empty Stomach

My psychiatrist prescribed
medicine for my anxiety to
take orally.

I'm supposed to take one
to two tablets a day as needed
if I'm feeling anxious.

Now, if I don't take
my anxiety medication, I have
anxiety about not taking it.

Page Nineteen

If you open the black book of poems
sitting on the third row of the bookshelf
in my study
& turn to page nineteen,
you'll see a bright red splatter of blood
on the upper right corner of the page—
just above the title of the poem.

I killed a mosquito
that landed on the book
while I was reading on my porch.

The blood is mine,
I think.

Cock Fighting for the Rich

Step right up, Sir!

*Welcome to the other side
of the tracks!*

*Check out this fine lineup
of young men we have here!*

What does this one do?

*Can he shoot a ball?
What about dribbling?*

Let me see. Let me see.

No. OK, OK, OK.

*What about throwing?
Can he throw one?*

No. OK, OK, OK.

*What about catching?
Can he catch one?*

No. OK, OK, OK.

*What can he do for us?
Let me see. Let me see.*

Give him a gun.

Patriotic Justice

Enlisted after school.
A funny thing to do for
a pacifist, right?

Mend the Fence

My girlfriend
asked me
to take
out the
trash so
I took
out the
trash &
then sat
on the
back porch
& smoked
a joint.
Hope she
doesn't come
outside.
She told
me to quit.
I should
probably fix
the fence.

Celebrating a New Milestone

I'm happy to share
I've started a new role
as a guy who smokes
weed & writes poetry.

Twenty-three
people
like this
& two others
find it insightful.

Sharon said congrats
with the clapping hand
emoji.

Final Boss

I should probably go to
the gym, but I think I'll
just stay home,
play video games
& masturbate.

There's a new level
I've been trying to reach,
but I can't get past
this one boss.

Wallet, Phone, Keys

Wallet is on my desk next
to the laptop. I was
ordering pizza earlier &
they had a deal that was
only available online.

Phone is sitting on the right arm
of the couch. I must have picked
it up & checked my social
media forty-seven times tonight.

Where the fuck are my keys,
it's too cold outside to walk to
the drive-thru again.

This Stinks

I planted a flowering dogwood
where an old tree stump used to be.

It's been three months & the leaves
are beginning to die.

The trunk hasn't gotten any thicker.
I don't think the tree is going to make it.
I'm not very good at this stuff.

Get Them Wet and They Thrive

I don't know why
I wait until
my plants are
almost
dead
to water them.

Coffee Maker

I went to the convenience store
to get a cup of coffee.
The attendant said – *the Powerball
is up to 1.1 billion.*

I told him, *no thanks-*
I don't gamble.

My dad keeps telling me
to get a coffee maker
to save some money,
but then I'd have to
brew it every day.

Product Placement

I walked downtown
to the bar
to have a few drinks.

Figured if I walked there,
I couldn't drive home.

After a couple hours,
I called an Uber
to take me home.

Ten minutes later,
when I got home,
I grabbed my keys
& drove to the drive thru
to get some snacks.

The drive thru
had six packs of IPAs
on sale for $9.99.

Never could pass up
a good sale.

Blowout

Hit a pothole
on my way
home from work.

Had to get the car
towed.

Should I tell
her about that
or that I lost my job?

Which one should
I explain first?

I'm too high
for this right now.

Restaurantification

Put a fancy name
on your restaurant.

It's still next to the hardware store
on the west side
at the outlet mall.

You can't keep charging
these ridiculous prices.

We know what it is.

You're not the first person that tried.

Seller's Market

The house next door
sold above
asking price.

I thought
maybe
mine
would be
worth that much.

But theirs is
updated
& a little
bigger
than mine.

Leaky Pipes

What do you do,
she asked.

I'm a poet, I replied.

So, you're unemployed.

Oh, you mean what do
I do for money,
I suggested.

I don't identify as
a plumber.

Open To Work

Hi, everyone!
After four
great months &
a successful stint
at my last gig,
I'm sad to say
I was impacted
by the most
recent round
of layoffs &
I'm seeking
my next
grand
fucking
adventure.

Beer Snob

The man sat down at the bar
& asked the bartender what
IPAs she has on tap,
as if to suggest he doesn't know.

The bartender names the ones
she knows offhand & then
grabs the draft list & brings it to him.

The man orders the first beer.

"*Is this a local?*" he asked.

"*Yes,*" she says. "*It's right across town.*"

The man already knew that.
He's had that one before.

Before the man has a chance
to finish his first beer,
she asks if he'd like another one.

The man asks
what other IPAs
she has on tap.

"*Let me try the other one,*" he says.

As if to suggest he's only drinking
them for the taste & to try something new.

Bobbi

I wish I had one night
with Bobbi Althoff.

Not so I could sleep with her.

So she could ask me
questions about my life &
tell me how stupid I am.

I'm into that kind of shit.

Heavy Weight, Low Reps

Damn, she lights up a room.
That body is crazy. She definitely
MUST do hip thrusts every day.

We could go together, honestly.

Baby! Baby! Baby! - I thought.

I'll just go say hi. No, wait! I have
to think of something clever first.

I know - I'll ask her for workout
advice & pretend I don't know
what I'm doing. (I really don't.

I walked towards her & before
I couldn't get the words out I'd
been practicing from across the
room...

Eww - she said.
Get away from
me, you creep.

Something about a First Kiss

Sitting at my favorite bar alone
on a Wednesday night,
hoping to meet someone new.
Staring across the room when I
noticed her for the first time.
She looked at me only for
a second, then sat two seats
down to the left, leaving a seat
between us as if she were guarding
herself from getting hurt again.
I thought I'd say hello and ask her
name. I looked away for a second
to get the bartender's attention.
When I turned back around, a man
came up behind her and kissed her
forehead before sitting between us.

Until We Meet Again

I bought two wooden
Adirondack chairs
for my front porch.
I guess I'm being optimistic.

Breathtaking

Lying in bed.
I could feel my body
waking up for the day.

I opened my eyes.
The view was breathtaking.

There she lies.

Watching her sleep
is the most beautiful
thing I've ever witnessed.

Until she opens her mouth.

Her breath smells awful.

Good Girl

Last night
I had
a one-night stand
with the
type
of woman
I would bring
home
to meet my mother

Real Freaky Shit

I like a freaky chick
real nasty like
educated & well spoken
communicates effectively
respects my mother
supports my dreams
a freaky ass chick
real nasty

Suns Out, Buns Out

Sometimes I like
to lay in bed
with my dogs
while the sun
is still out

Pawshank Redemption

Iron bars confining not
just my physical being
but my spirit & my
conscious.

How did I get here?

What could I have
done differently?

If only I hadn't pee'd
on the carpet in the
family room.

My dog probably

Hurt My Pride

I got my
ass beat
by a
butch
lesbian.

She was
a good
friend
of mine.

I'm About to Bust

Oh my god, bro.
Oh my god, bro.
I need you.

Oh my god, bro.
Behind me.

Grab that shit.
Grab that shit.
Pick that up.

I'm coming.
I'm coming.
I'm coming.

Babe! Don't you think you're
too old to be playing Fortnite?

Come watch a movie with me.

There's Something About Sherry

All day I stood in the blistering cold
outside the payphone on 5th & Main.

My fingers started to go numb.
Legs shaking from standing so long.
Lips purple. Cheeks red as could be.

The moment I leave for warmth and comfort could be the moment
you call, so I'll wait here a while longer. You're worth it.

The phone finally rang. I rushed over and
opened the door of the phone booth,
barely answering it in time - or so it felt.

"Hello! Hello! Sherry, is that you?" I asked
frantically.

The voice on the other side replied:

"Hi! We've been trying to reach you
about your car's extended warranty…"

F1-Racing

Lying in my bed
awake.

I've got a million
thoughts
in my head I'm
trying
to get out.

Kingda Ka *(Haiku)*

depression lurking
frenzy of mania gone
half-finished projects

Eat Your Vegetables

My dad is
coming
over later.
I better go
buy some
groceries
so he
doesn't
think I'm
eating out
everyday.

Candy Painted Hearse, Sitting on 22s

cruising down the interstate
heading down to *chik-fil-a*
speeding in the fast lane
oh no it's sunday
my blood sugar is fifty-eight
may as well crash this ford escape

Drug Dealers on Every Corner

Trying to
get
out of
the habit
of eating
fast food
everyday.

I think
they
designed
it this way.

Prescription Tattoo

Maybe
I should
get a
face tat
to show
the
world
my
anxiety
is real

It Only Stings at First

A large wasp was buzzing
around my head.

I pushed em away
so it wouldn't get hurt.

I tend to do that.

Spray Bottle Full of Round-up

There's a dandelion
growing
through the crack
of the broken
concrete
in the driveway.

I'll let it grow
awhile.

Deserves
a chance
just like
the rest
of us.

Kanye

Laying in a field
of dandelions
staring up at the stars
that one cloud
to the northwest
looks like
one of the Kardashians

Groundhog's Day

I bought a fishing pole today.

Something about a fall breeze
inspired my curiosity.

I cannot keep living inside
with the shutters closed.

How I long to experience
something new again.

I cannot keep living the same
way I lived yesterday,
& the day before.

Something has to give.

I begin to thread the line
on my new fishing pole in
the driveway. The line was
tangled & wouldn't thread
so easily.

Oh well, I guess
I'll try again tomorrow.

Coulda Been Fishing

Thunderstorm.
Torrential downpour.

That's ok.

I'll stay inside &
watch Druski.

I wasn't planning
on going anywhere
anyways.

Algorithm

Botox
Boob job
Filler
Ass shots

Thirst traps
DMs
First dates
Back shots

Long Term, Open to Short

Why are you
asking me
if I'm open to kids?

Did you not read
my fucking bio?

Colonoscopy *(Haiku)*

Workout anytime
24-7 fitness
Still eating fast food

Sailor Town *(Haiku)*

Ouch! That fucking hurt
Baby don't bite my nipples
It's freezing in here

FOMO *(Haiku)*

Texting & driving
Checking social media
Fear of missing out

James Dolan

going bowling
hand holding
baby strolling
heart broken
house sold in
minnesota
clogged colon
joint rolling
blunt toking
gun smoking
golden token

whewwww –
fingerguns.

My Cool Uncle Buys Me Snacks

My mom & dad
did the best they
could to raise me.

They turned
it over to my Uncle
Sam after they
couldn't take it
anymore.

He was there
for my dad too
when he was
younger.

Greener Pastures

My friend since grade school
calls me every now and then.

He talks about bachelor life.

I talk about settling down.

Neither of us will ever know.

Apple of Her Eye

A young mother waited patiently
outside the principal's office
with the school secretary.

This was the third time this week
she had to leave work early to tend
to her young son.

He started three fights at school
that week & lost every one of them.

You'll Always Be My Brother *(Haiku)*

Harrelson and Snipes.
Starsky and Hutch. Hook and Worm.
SpongeBob and Patrick.

Dear Charles

Thank you
for showing me
the world
for what it truly is.

A beautiful place
where despite all
our faults,
we can all
coexist.

Poe Me Another One

Did the word *poet*
derive from
Edgar Allen Poe?

This shit is hitting.

Empty water jugs.
Red hostel rooftop.
Two curfew violations.
Nagasaki boys.

You can't lay in bed
& masturbate to Reddit
all fucking day, bro.

Well, That Escalated Quickly

ordered a cold brew
from the canteen
make it venti
leave room for cream

got my coffee
filled with glee
until I noticed
there was no cream

I opened the lid
to add half & half
hand slipped on the lid
poured in my lap

missed my interview
to go home and change
mortgage is behind
what will it take

lost the house
when will it stop
If only the barista
did his fucking job

Butterfly Effect

A girl cut her left wrist
& butterflies flew out.

Her mother put on her best dress.

A black dress with a matching hat
covering her face.

A good thing as
she weeps into her handkerchief,
hoping no one notices.

She never was one for making a scene.

A boy is playing music, as
the preacher talks about the beauty
of a life taken too soon.

A butterfly flies by the woman
& grazes her left ear
before flying off into the sunset.

Money Laundering

I forgot I went
to the strip club
last night
until I washed
my laundry

There was
a one-dollar bill
for every
article of clothing

Pepperoni & Cheese

All my friends
are getting married
& having kids
while I sit on
the couch in my
boxers with my dog
eating pizza

KJ Lay Down

It's 1:57 AM lying in bed.

My dog is snoring.

He just farted.

His big hairy ass
is right next
to my pillowcase.

I can't sleep
under these conditions.

Guilt Trip

I had a dream I was going 72 down
I-75 South & hit an elderly man driving
a motorized scooter crossing the freeway.

Woke up in a cold sweat.

Thankfully, it was just a dream.

Virginia Beach

last weekend
I drove to the ocean
just to stare
across the water
dreaming you were
on the other side
staring back at me
until a jellyfish
stung my big toe
I had to limp
back to my car

Sharpen the Blade

Your words cut
like a dull knife
slicing through butter,
she said.

Why do I always
sabotage
my happiness?

Hello Again, My Old Friend

open the door
to let you out

cut you
in two pieces

caress you
between my
fingers

take you
at my will

sit
& watch
the cars
pass by

the stars come out

there you are,
old friend –

i've missed you.

Community Service

I started volunteering
at a nursing home
to get out of the house
& do something positive.

Thought it might help
my self-esteem a bit.

My first day volunteering,
an elderly woman challenged
me to a game of pickleball.
I let her win the first game.

She cheered as she raised
her arms victoriously.

I smiled a bit.
She asked me to run it back
& started shit talking me.

I decided to take things seriously.
I didn't mean to hit the ball so hard.
I hope her family understands.

New Journey, New Beginning

"I'm proud to say
after a yearlong search,
thousands of applications,
hundreds of rejection letters,
I've decided I honestly don't
give a fuck anymore."

— Random HR pro sipping a Matcha Latte at the local coworking space, trying to hold the tears back, while swearing she's starting her own consulting business.

Will Work for Food

I started
writing
poetry
to find
a home
for the
thoughts
in my head.

It only
created
more
homeless
thoughts.

Unchained

Now that
everyone
knows
I'm bipolar
I can go
& live
my life

                           Ta-ta for now.

Meet The Author

Brandon Sites resides in Miamisburg, Ohio, with his two dogs, KJ and Peanut. When he's not writing, he enjoys playing basketball, thrifting, café hopping, cheering on Ohio sports and doing home improvement projects.

Brandon served on active duty in the United States Navy as a Master at Arms for seven years. During his service, Brandon was a responding officer involved in a military base shooting and was later medically retired from service with a diagnosis of post-traumatic stress disorder.

Two years after being honorably discharged, Brandon was diagnosed with bipolar disorder. Determined to prove he was more than his diagnosis, Brandon graduated *Cum Laude* with a Bachelor of Arts in Management from American Military University and a Master of Business Administration from Eastern University.

Brandon then had a short stint in the corporate world before founding his own publishing company, choosing to instead write and focus on his mental health.

He found healing through writing.

Upcoming title:

Bury Me in Appalachia

A collection of poetry exploring themes of working-class life in rural America.

www.ingramcontent.com/pod-product-compliance
Lightning Source LLC
Chambersburg PA
CBHW020420150626
46554CB00014B/2253